GOOD
KARMA

GOOD KARMA

MAKE THE RIGHT CHOICES

FOR TOMORROW

JAYA ROW

HarperCollins *Publishers* India

First published in paperback in India by
HarperCollins *Publishers* in 2021
A-75, Sector 57, Noida, Uttar Pradesh 201301, India
www.harpercollins.co.in

2 4 6 8 10 9 7 5 3 1

P-ISBN: 978-93-9035-191-6
E-ISBN: 978-93-9035-192-3

Typeset in 12/18.4 Giovanni Book at
Manipal Technologies Limited, Manipal

Printed and bound at
Thomson Press (India) Ltd.

To the Gurus

Contents

SECTION IV: The Way Out

Introduction

The world has been facing an unprecedented challenge since the beginning of 2020. Uncertainty is all around us. It is when life throws a curveball at you that you wonder – do things happen randomly? Is life like a game of roulette or is there a method in the madness? Are we completely powerless, mere victims of fate, or do we have some say in determining life's course? Do we have any control over what is happening around us and to us? It seems as if not everything is under our control. Yet, we are not entirely powerless. As a thinker said, 'We cannot always choose the music life plays for us but we can choose how we dance to it.' In this lies our hope.

The word 'karma' is often used loosely, without understanding its depth. People dismiss incidents that occur in their lives as 'my karma', suggesting that it is just their bad luck. It indicates helplessness and lack of power. Karma is anything but a passive submission to fate.

The ancient Indian sages have left an impressive body of study and research done on the subject of karma. It is exhaustive, systematic and complete. It is based on scientific data they collected and analysed, connecting seemingly unconnected facts and arriving at irrefutable conclusions. They discovered the Law of Karma. The source is in the Upanishads, the last portion of each of the Vedas. Great thinkers down the ages investigated independently on the subject and arrived at the same conclusions. They explained how the law of cause and effect that operates in the external world also functions in the inner world of thought, attitude and intention that manifest as action.

Once you understand the law, you can use it to your advantage to achieve your purpose, your goal, in life. Things become clear. You realize that everything in life is a reflection of the choices you have made in the past. To bring about a more successful and happier result, you now have to make different choices. The power lies in you. You are not a puppet in the hands of an unknown entity. You have the power to create your own destiny. With this new-found confidence, you begin to sculpt a brilliant future for yourself.

SECTION I

Fate Versus Free Will

1

Laws that Govern the Inner World

Human suffering is one of life's most compelling mysteries. Why does one person have a smooth journey through life, while another faces more than his share of problems? Why is one person born with a silver spoon in the mouth and another born in a slum? Is the Creator partial? Are we mere puppets in the hands of an unknown puppeteer? Or do we have the power to mould our own future? What governs the course of our lives? Is it fate? Are our life paths predetermined by a higher power? Or is there a thing called free will that we can use to chart our own course through life? These are some of the questions that baffle us.

Philosophers, thinkers and religious leaders have deliberated over 'fate versus free will' for ages. The early Greeks thought that the inescapable destiny of each individual was preordained by supernatural powers known as 'gods'. Later, philosophers like Plato and Aristotle brought a more rational view. The concept of free will was connected to moral responsibility. They felt that our actions depend more on us and are less predetermined by fate. However, the belief prevailed that the course of destiny is already charted out for the individual. Even if he chooses another alternative, he would meet with similar consequences in the long run. Modern thinkers are more inclined towards the idea of free will, but the debate continues to rage.

On the one hand, there are those who believe in fate. They believe that God has created the universe and is, therefore, responsible for all that happens in it. Everything that happens in everyone's life is God's will. Everyone's life is written before birth, and there is nothing anyone can do to alter it.

On the other hand, there are those who believe in free will. They believe that each individual is entirely responsible for his own life and has the power to create his own destiny. There is no God and no such thing as luck. Then, of course, there are those in the middle. This group believes that our lives are a combination of fate and free will. The story below illustrates the saying 'God helps those who help themselves'.

The Old Man and the Storm

An old man once had a dream that a storm would come and wipe away his village, but that God would protect him. As it happened, they had a terrible storm in the village the next day.

The old man's brother told him to leave the village as things were getting worse. He refused, saying God would protect him. On the second day, a neighbour came saying he was leaving with his family and offered to take the old man along. The old man declined because he was sure that God would protect him. On the third day, some people came on a boat and offered to take him to safety.

Again, the old man refused, convinced that God would protect him.

Soon after, the man drowned and was taken to heaven. There, he asked God: 'Why didn't you help me as you had promised?' God replied: 'I sent your brother, your neighbour and even a boat to take you to safety. You refused all three times!'

The question remains: How do we fulfil our life's purpose if we don't even know whether we are governed by fate or free will?

Fortunately, in ancient India, scientific thinkers focused on the inner world and discovered laws that govern our minds, in the same way that scientists discovered laws pertaining to the material world. If we understand these laws and abide by them, we can live happy, successful and fulfilled lives.

2

The Law of Karma

J ust as Newton wondered what made an apple fall down to earth and eventually discovered the law of gravity, ancient sages in India pondered over life and its various mysteries. They discovered the law of causation – that every cause has an effect and every effect must have had a cause.

There are many laws that function in the inner world. Understand what they are and how they function, so you can use them to your advantage. One such law is the Law of Karma.

Christianity and Islam ascribe heaven as the
fruit of good actions and hell as punishment for
bad actions. In modern times, more people in the
West have started believing in the Law of Karma in
some way. Psychologists and psychiatrists are using
past-life regression to help their patients recover
from the effects of trauma from past lives. Dr Brian
Weiss, a Columbia- and Yale-trained psychiatrist,
has contributed immensely to the field of Past-
Life Regression. He is called the 'Father of Modern
Past-Life Regression'. Dr Ian Stevenson, Dr Michael
Newton and others are among the well-known
practitioners who have written books based on
their research.

The pre-Vedic masters may have understood the
Law of Karma, but it was first documented and
explained in the Upanishads. It is the very basis of
the spiritual path that leads us from the mortal life
of sorrow and suffering to the immortal state of
infinite Bliss. The Brihadaranyaka Upanishad, the
Shvetashvatara Upanishad and many others refer
to the Law of Karma, which includes the theory
of reincarnation. The Bhagavad Gita speaks of it
in almost every chapter and explicitly explains the

concept of reincarnation in Chapter 2, Verse 22, which says:

Vasamsi jirnani yatha vihaya
Navani grhnati naroparani
Tatha sharirani vihaya jirna-
Nyanyani samyati navani dehi
As a person abandons tattered clothes to don new ones, so the inner personality abandons jaded bodies to enter new ones.

It further explains that the thoughts we entertain and actions we perform determine not only our future in this lifetime but also the birth and environment one goes to after death. The doctrine of Karma was later accepted in Jainism, Buddhism as well as Sikhism.

The power of thought and its ability to change the course of life is highlighted in Indian scriptures. Epics like the Ramayana and Mahabharata as well as the Puranas speak of the role of karma or action in determining life's journey.

Consider the reincarnation story of Shikhandi in the Mahabharata. Shikhandi was Amba, the daughter of the king of Kashi in an earlier birth.

Amba, along with her sisters, Ambika and Ambalika, were brought by Bhishma to marry Vichitravirya, his half-brother. Amba said she was already in love with another king so Bhishma sent her to him. But he refused to marry Amba as she had already been taken elsewhere. Amba blamed Bhishma for her situation and vowed to kill him in revenge. Amba was born as Shikhandini, daughter of Drupada. She changed her gender to become Shikhandi and killed Bhishma in the Mahabharata war.

The Law of Karma is the overarching law that applies universally to all human beings. It states that every thought, emotion or action has an equal and opposite reaction. It is infallible, like the law of gravity. Ignorance of the law does not exempt you from its effect. To commit an act and hope to get away with it is like dropping a stone in water and expecting no ripples. It would be prudent, therefore, to know what the repercussions of your actions would be, so that you can decide how to act in order to get the result you want.

KARMA - ACTION

PIVOT AROUND WHICH LIFE REVOLVES

Karma comes from the Sanskrit root *kr*, which means 'to do'. Action is the pivot around which life revolves. Every volitional act has a result. Driven by greed, hatred and selfishness, you plant seeds of suffering and misery. Motivated by generosity, love and wisdom, you create abundance and happiness for yourself. Once an apple seed is planted it will bear apples, not mangoes. No amount of beseeching, manipulation or bargaining will produce mangoes. The only way to get mangoes is by planting a mango seed. Similarly, if you want happiness, you need to sow the requisite seeds.

Cultivate a charitable mindset, be loving and forgiving, gain clarity of thought. And happiness will be the result. You cannot be hateful, vicious and negative and expect to be happy. People think, feel and act recklessly, without regard to the consequences, and when the result comes, they complain! It is like going to a restaurant and ordering a dish, but when it is brought to the table, you say you do not want it. You can choose not to eat it but pay for it you must.

People do not see the law operating in life and attribute their problems to external factors that have no connection to the situation they are in. Thus, the situation never changes. It reappears in some other form somewhere else. Over and over again.

3

As You Think So You Become

The law of life is, 'As you think so you become.' All change or improvement begins with a thought. A thought occurs to you. You invest in it. You begin to see the same thing from a different perspective. Your attitude changes. You act in line with your changed perception. And the situation miraculously transforms. This happens at an individual level as well as at community, national and international planes.

For 200 years, Indians were content to have the British rule over them. A few people began questioning and said, 'Swaraj is my birthright and

I will have it.' This thought spread, and soon India gained Independence.

The great Emperor Ashoka was the last major emperor of the Mauryan dynasty. He conquered Kalinga, modern-day Odisha, in a bloody war. The suffering that the battle inflicted on the defeated people moved him to such remorse that he renounced armed conquests. He adopted Buddhism. Under its influence and prompted by his own dynamic temperament, he resolved to live by dharma and to serve his subjects and all humanity. He adopted a policy that he called 'conquest by dharma'.

Traditional non-vegetarians, who ate meat at every meal, turned vegan or vegetarian when they became aware of the immense torture that animals were subjected to, the harm the meat industry caused to the environment, and its ill effects on their health.

So can you bring mind-blowing changes in life by just changing your thoughts. Think thin, you become slim. Think smart, you become sharp. Think activity, and you overcome sloth. Attributing your misfortune to the stars will neither change your life nor alleviate your suffering. When adversity and hardship come your way, you can blame your spouse, boss or the government, or look at the situation proactively. As long as you are blaming someone outside, your situation will never improve. You have no control over others. The moment you look within, miracles happen.

You may have always wanted to lose weight. Start thinking fit and slim, you develop a strong desire for it and begin acting in that direction. Your lifestyle changes and the result is so gratifying. You may have been jealous of your colleague or sibling. You begin to see that she has worked hard to be where she is. You shift from harbouring jealous and negative thoughts to building your own merit. You work hard and achieve what you always wanted to attain.

So take a look at your thoughts. They are the blueprint of your life. Thought by thought, you can build a great life. Thought by thought, you can destroy yourself. Identify what agitates you, what causes you grief and anxiety. Change your mindset. Tweak your thoughts. And your life becomes happy and peaceful.

Suppose you are watching a movie on a screen and suddenly notice a black spot on the cheek of the hero. The spot then moves to the floor, the car and other objects in the movie. You try and remove the black spot by wiping the screen, washing it and even changing it. The black spot persists. This is because the cause of the spot is not on the screen but on the projector. There is a small speck of dust on the lens of the projector. All you have to do is wipe the lens and the spot is gone.

Similarly, all problems are in the mind. You only have to make a slight shift in thinking and the problem disappears from the world. It is as simple as that. There is insecurity, lack of self-sufficiency, superiority or inferiority complex, sibling rivalry and other baggage from the past that is weighing you down. Get down to the job of cleansing the dirt within, rehabilitating your inner personality and transforming yourself. Instead, you change your spouse, separate from your business partner, relocate to another city or country. For a while things are fine, but soon issues crop up. You are back to square one.

As long as you look outward and blame something or someone out there for your ills, you will never be free from the pain and suffering you are subjecting yourself to. Look within and you will see the areas that are causing you grief. Enrich yourself internally and the wealth of the world will be at your feet. You will be a happy person and grow into a towering personality.

For years, East and West Germany were enemies. They spent a large part of their resources on fighting each other. Then there was a change of heart. They began to understand that they would be a far more prosperous and powerful nation united, rather than separate. The famous Berlin wall crashed. But not before the wall was brought down in their minds.

India, Pakistan and Bangladesh were one nation until we started creating differences in our minds. This led to the creation of two nations, and then three. If we think one, we will become united again – resurgent, prosperous, powerful. The verse from the Rig Veda, which is the basis of the Indian ethos and mindset, says:

Ayam nijah param veti ganana laghuchetasam
Udaracharitanam tu vasudhaiva kutumbakam
Small-minded people differentiate between
mine and yours. Large-hearted people believe
the entire universe is one family.

President Barack Obama had quoted this verse
when he had addressed the Indian parliament. We
need to reinstate it in our hearts and minds.

Not living this concept tears apart couples,
families, organizations as well as nations.
People who have been together for decades,
sometimes generations, start thinking of divisions,
demarcations and separateness, leading to a painful
parting of ways and financial as well as emotional
loss. Whereas people who have been at war for
generations can bring peace and prosperity into
their lives by thinking afresh.

Two brothers were fighting over assets for years.
Eventually, they decided to appoint arbitrators to
resolve the conflict. The older brother chose his
arbitrator and asked the younger one to name his.
The younger one said he wanted the older brother
to be his arbitrator as he could not think of a better

person than him to look after his interests. The separation never happened.

Look for the common denominator. Focus on the positives, make up for deficiencies. Find an inspiring goal that will bring people together. Work for *lokasangraha*, the wellbeing of the world. People will come together in a spirit of camaraderie, fun and cheer. And magical results will follow.

SECTION II

Thoughts and Actions

4

The Power of Your Thoughts

There is a story in the Bhagavatam of a great monarch Bharata. In his old age, he gave up his life of luxury and opulence, handed over the kingdom to his son and retired to the forest. It is said that Bharata was then on the verge of Enlightenment. One day when he was in deep meditation, a hunter who was chasing a pregnant deer came in the vicinity. As the deer delivered the offspring, the hunter killed her.

Bharata saw that the infant would die without help so he looked after it. In the process, he got attached to the baby deer. Instead of thinking of

God, his thoughts would go to the deer and he would wonder if the deer was all right. Even on his deathbed, his attention was on the deer. As a result, the desire for the deer that he had cultivated made him go through an entire incarnation as a deer before he got enlightened. This is the frightening power of thought. Not knowing this, we carelessly entertain all kinds of thoughts, oblivious of their effects.

Your thoughts are the building blocks of life. Every thought delivers an unseen chisel blow in shaping your future. The mind is the master architect of both the inner blueprint of character and personality as well as the outer structure of situation and environment. Your thoughts determine whether your mind is tranquil or agitated. They decide the clarity or confusion of the intellect. And the body follows suit. If you are heedless of health, you eat the wrong type of food and suffer from all sorts of ailments. The moment you become aware of healthy living, you eat nutritious food, exercise and become fit and strong. It is ignorance that makes you act against your interests. Once you become aware, correction is automatic.

Osho said: 'Why are you doing silly things? Because you are not aware of what you are doing.' The moment you become aware you will automatically stop being foolish. So, first become aware of your thoughts, emotions and actions. Understand the impact they have on your life. And you will stop doing the things that cause you grief.

If the blueprint is drawn in ignorance, the mind creates pain and suffering for you. Shaped in knowledge, it creates a life of joy and happiness. In the armoury of thoughts, you have the power to sculpt weapons of self-destruction or create pathways to self-development. The choice is yours. Thus, you are the designer of your character, the builder of your life and the creator of your destiny. There is no outside agency that has the power to influence your passage through life.

Your life is like a movie being projected on the screen. The screen is the world. The film consisting of individual pictures is your mind and the pictures are your thoughts. The light in the projector is the subtle, inconceivable Spirit that enables all of this.

When the film moves at a certain speed, it projects life on the screen. You see it out there but understand its origin is in the film. Similarly, when thoughts move at a certain speed in the mind, it projects a reality out there that is life-like. You find it difficult to believe that it is a mere projection. It is, nevertheless, true.

When a person thinks of trading in stocks, he becomes a stockbroker. His mind then projects a world of stocks and shares. Another person thinks of medicine and becomes a doctor. Thereafter, the hospital, patients, nurses and other doctors form her world. If you think of music, you become a musician and create a world of music, performances and creativity. Think cooking and you are in a world of food. Thus it goes on. Thought is the ultimate cause of your environment.

If you are not happy with your world, you cannot go out there and change things. It is as absurd as changing the screen when you want to watch a different movie. You are only positioning yourself for failure and disappointment. All you have to do is change the film and enjoy the movie of your choice. Similarly, change your thoughts, make a shift in attitude, alter your feelings. The world miraculously changes!

In the end, when there is no film in the projector, the movie on the screen comes to an end. When the mind becomes free of desire, there is no world projected. You become the Spirit. You reach the abode of peace and bliss.

Decide what you want to achieve in life, figure out how to get there and start working towards it. Watch your thoughts, control them, trace their effects. To sit back and blame your stars, your parents or the environment is futile. Opportunities will not fall in your lap. You have to create them for yourself.

The absurdity of the situation is that having created your own world, you are traumatized by it. One person is stressed out, another fearful and yet another miserable. You have created a Frankenstein's monster that is now devouring you.

This happens because we fall for the trap of instant pleasure. Everyone wants success, happiness and fulfilment here and now. Nobody is prepared to wait. However, the law of life, spelt out clearly in the Bhagavad Gita, Chapter 18, Verse 36, is:

vishayendriya samyogadyat tadagre'mrtopamam
pariname vishamiva tat sukham rajasam smrtam

False happiness, arising from sense contact,
is like nectar in the beginning but like poison
in the end.

On the other hand, Bhagavad Gita, Chapter 18,
Verse 37 says:

yattadagre vishamiva pariname'mrtopamam
tat sukham sattvikam proktam atma buddhiprasadajam
That happiness is real, born of the purity of
one's intellect, which is like poison in the
beginning but nectar in the end.

Pleasures born of sense contact have a beginning
and an end. They are wombs of sorrow. The wise do
not indulge in them. True happiness, which comes
from the purity of the intellect, is painful in the
beginning but yields immense bliss in the end. Not
knowing this, you opt for instant joys, signing up
for a lifetime of sorrow.

Junk food is so tasty that a child automatically
gravitates towards it. Healthy food often can be
distasteful. If you eat junk food all the time, you end

up with all kinds of health issues. To laze and not exercise is so pleasurable. To pull yourself out of bed to exercise is agonizing. But if you make that effort you become fit, healthy and energetic.

It gives a weird sense of satisfaction when you are nasty, rude and hurtful to people, but you end up disliked, miserable and lonely. It requires effort to rein in your negativities and be affectionate and loving towards others, but that makes for a happy life. For a few seconds of pleasure, we give up a lifetime of happiness! So, understand the law and abide by it to create a life of peace and happiness. This does not mean that you have to lead a boring life. Just think before you do things. Help yourself to instant joys. But also invest in your own long-term interests.

There was a kingdom that had a strange practice. A king would be chosen every five years. At the end of his tenure, the king would be ferried across the river to be devoured by wild animals in the jungle on the other bank. King after king came. Every man enjoyed his wealth, power and stature for the first few years but as time passed, he was tormented by the fate that awaited him. The fifth year was torture. On the last day, he had to be forced out of the palace and placed in the boat that took him to his death.

Once, a king was appointed who was different from the rest. With every passing year, his revelry and enjoyment increased. On the last day of his monarchy, he threw a magnificent banquet for all the citizens, waved goodbye to them and stepped into the boat. When the boat was halfway across, he looked at the boatman and asked him if he would be willing to work for him if he doubled his salary. The boatman was confused. He wondered if the king was offering him a job in heaven. Just then they reached the other shore and the boatman was astonished to see a magnificent city there in place of the wild jungle. The king, in his wisdom, had systematically transferred his assets from the state in which he was the temporary king to the other shore, where he would be king forever.

Similarly, we all have a temporary sojourn in life. At least the king had five years assured to him. We do not have even five minutes guaranteed to us. Yet, we do not think of the afterlife. By all means, enjoy what the world has to offer. Go shopping in the malls of the world, travel to exotic locations, sip the finest wines and eat the most exquisite food. But do not forget to invest a little time in building your inner reserves, which you will carry forward with you. Develop clarity of thought, purity of heart and sincerity of action that will assure you a life of prosperity, happiness and growth. What is the use of being a billionaire in this life if, after death, you are born in a slum not far from your luxurious mansion!

You are born with a mix of desires that make your personality. Some are good, others not so good. If you create an environment of powerful positive thoughts in your mind, the good tendencies in you will flourish and blossom while the bad ones will fade away without your having to put in much effort. This is called *satsang* or the company of the good.

Satsang is not just hanging around a good person. It is making a conscious effort to cultivate positive thoughts and steering clear of negativities. Read uplifting books, not pulp fiction. Expose yourself to spiritual thoughts and literature on a daily basis. 'Read not Times, read Eternities,' said a thinker. Don't miss the pun on 'Times'. Do not watch the news. Breaking news only breaks you! Watch inspiring movies. Keep away from gossipmongers. This is the foundation on which you build the edifice of your life.

5

Vasanas Versus Choice of Action

What is the source of action? Over the weekend, you may go to a music concert, your spouse may watch a movie on Netflix, your son may go to a soccer match and your daughter may choose to hang out with friends. Why do different people act differently? Because they have a desire for it. Action is preceded by desire. You perform action because you have a desire for it.

How is desire born? Desire arises from thought. At some point, the thought occurred to you. Why did you get that particular thought? Because you have a *vasana* for it. Vasana is a deep-rooted interest, inherent urge, inclination or tendency. Vasana is latent, unmanifest desire. A person with musical vasanas will think of music, one with vasana for soccer will think of soccer and so on. As you invest in the thought, you develop a desire for it and you fulfil the desire through action. Action driven by desire then results in more vasana. Thus, you are bound in the loop of vasana, thought, desire, action and again vasana.

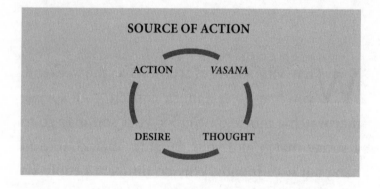

As is your vasana, so will be the thought, desire, action as well as circumstance. An engineer will think of buildings and bridges, develop a desire for making them and actually make that his profession. He will then surround himself with other engineers.

Likewise, a criminal will find himself in the company of other crooks and a good person will be with noble people.

Circumstances do not make a man, they reveal him. The environment is a reflection of your mind. If you want to change your world, you cannot go out and change the circumstances directly. All you have to do is modify your thoughts. And the circumstances will automatically alter.

A lazy person wasting time, binge-watching movies and eating unhealthy snacks will have friends who do similar things. When he decides to become fit, he starts exercising, going to the gym and eating healthy food. Mysteriously, his erstwhile friends disappear and he finds himself in the company of people who enjoy a healthy life and are on a mission to keep fit. Similarly, entertain positive thoughts, feel loving emotions and commit yourself to a higher goal and your world improves dramatically.

In *Les Miserables* by Victor Hugo, the convict Jean Valjean escapes from prison and is seeking shelter on a cold, wintry night. He finds that the bishop's door is not locked and enters. The bishop gives him food, wine and a warm bed to sleep in. The next morning, the convict steals the silverware from the bishop's home and disappears. The police find him and bring him back to the bishop, who protects him by saying he had gifted the silverware to him. As the convict is leaving, the bishop gives him gold candlesticks as well. This brings about a change in the convict's thinking and he starts doing great service to people. His attitude changes from grabbing to giving. He even becomes the mayor of the town.

Any change must begin with the mind. A person who wants to lose weight must first cultivate the value for fitness and good health. She must want to be fit and strong. The rest follows. An ill-tempered person must want to break free from the shackles of anger. A businessman who wants to come clean of corruption needs to understand the value of ethical business practices. A company that wants to go global can only do so when its leaders think global.

Destiny and Free Will

All beings act in accordance with their vasanas or nature. A cow is mild, a lion is ferocious, a deer is agile, and an elephant is slow. All creatures are bound by their nature. They do not have the freedom to change. A cow cannot become vicious. A lion does not have the option of developing compassion for its prey. A deer cannot choose to slow down. Each one is destined to live life according to its nature.

Human beings too have their nature and characteristic traits. There are aggressive people, gentle people, brilliant as well as dull ones. However, humans are the only species that have the power to change. Let us take a look at some examples.

There was once a diamond merchant named Shrinivasa Nayaka. One day, a poor man asked him for money. Shrinivasa Nayaka refused. The poor man then went to his wife, who gave him her nose ring. He went back to Shrinivasa Nayaka to pawn the nose ring. Shrinivasa recognized his wife's nose ring and questioned her about the secret donation.

Terrified at his anger, she rushed to consume poison, but found her nose ring in place of the poison! This changed Shrinivasa Nayaka, who donated his entire wealth and left home to become a mendicant.

He met Vyasatirtha Guru who introduced him to his musical talent and gave him the name Purandara Dasa. Purandara Dasa composed over 400,000 songs mostly in praise of Lord Vishnu. It is believed that the poor man who came begging for money was none other than Vishnu himself!

A beggar in Odisha started a school! He realized that his village did not have one. He started saving whatever he could from his earnings. When he had set aside enough from his income of begging, he started a school under a tree.

Steve Jobs, a college dropout, adopted by a working-class couple, struggled in the initial years. Yet, he rose to become one of the richest men in the world and made a significant impact on the lives of people worldwide.

There are millionaires who have become paupers, brilliant achievers who have turned criminal and so on. How does this work?

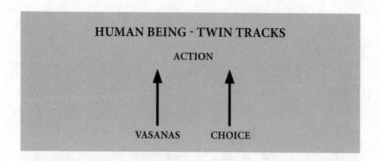

At the present moment, you are a victim of your vasanas. This is your fate, destiny or *prarabdha* – the sum total of all your past thoughts, desires and actions. This is irrevocable; it cannot change. It has its way. There is nothing you can do about it now.

However, every moment you have the wonderful gift of self-effort or *purushartha*, which is independent of destiny and completely under your control. So, you are free to choose every thought and action. Once the action is completed, you are a victim of its effect, which changes your destiny just that little bit. Consistent effort in a particular direction changes the course of your life.

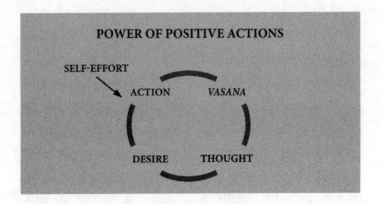

POWER OF POSITIVE ACTIONS

SELF-EFFORT

ACTION   *VASANA*

DESIRE   THOUGHT

As long as you think everything is predestined and beyond your control, you feel weak and powerless. You lose the motivation and zeal to act. When you realize that everything springs from you, you regain your confidence, zest and enthusiasm. It is in your power to create your destiny through free will. It takes awareness, passion, commitment and patience. Everyone is the master of his destiny.

When you find yourself in a negative situation, having to deal with a difficult spouse, financial loss or trying circumstances, the tendency is to blame the world and feel sorry for yourself. The truth is that the Law of Karma is operating and you had it coming to you. The other person or situation is a mere *nimitta*, or means, by which the law is panning out.

Look within. Trace back to the cause. Ask yourself if you could have handled things differently. Maybe it calls for an attitudinal shift, a slight change in the way you view things. Perhaps your conduct could do with a slight tweaking. When you have removed the cause of your misery, you find the environment also improves.

Until you look within and fix the cause, the same problem will recur in different ways, all your life, life after life. You perpetuate your misery unconsciously. You continue to be victimized by the world. So, take charge of your personality and make conscious choices towards a brighter future.

Viktor Frankl came out of a concentration camp without any animosity for the people who subjected him and others to intense torture and misery. When Nelson Mandela was released from decades in prison, he said if he did not leave behind the hatred and negativity, he would still be in that prison. However vicious the other person may be, if you refuse to think negatively, your life will change. The people who tortured Viktor Frankl and Nelson Mandela remained prison guards all their lives. Frankl and Mandela blossomed and grew into magnificent personalities, inspiring countless other people.

Find purpose. Fix a goal. Work towards it. When you have something inspiring to work for, you will not have the time or inclination to waste on negativities. Understand that everyone does what their nature dictates. Let them be. Feel sorry for their childishness. But refuse to get pulled down to their level.

Focus on your inspiration, your path, your mission. And life will change for you. As long as you allow the petty-minded evil people of the world to occupy your mind space, you are giving them unnecessary importance. You get bound to them. As a result, you are unable to enjoy your life. Learn the art of letting go.

Once, three ladies had invited a spiritual guru to lunch at an upmarket restaurant in London. Throughout the meal, they were busy speaking ill of their respective mothers-in-law. They were so involved in the discussion that nobody concentrated on the food. The guru kept quiet and enjoyed the delicious food instead. When he was done, he asked the ladies where their mothers-in-law were.

One said New York, the second Dubai and the third Hong Kong. The guru said, 'Why are you carrying the people you dislike so much to London? Let them be where they are and you enjoy your freedom.'

Often, it is just a case of lack of assessment, or improper assessment. Every individual has his or her own nature, just as animals have their distinct characteristics. An animal lover understands the nature of each animal and loves all animals. He adjusts to the nature of the animal and changes his behaviour accordingly. While he has the luxury of showering his affection on a pup or kitten, he shows love for the tiger or cobra in different ways. He does not expect the animal to adjust to his demands or expectations. Thus, he is happy with all creatures.

When it comes to dealing with human beings, this wisdom seems to elude us. Firstly, there is either incorrect or no understanding that people behave as per their nature and traits. You need to assess the nature of people, the climate, the city you live in and the government under which you live. Understand the nature of the world too. Just as a dog will bark, a snake will spit venom and a lion will pounce on innocent creatures, there are people who bark at you, are venomous towards you, or pounce on you. Understand, assess and accept. Then figure out how to deal with them.

Refuse to suffer for the other person's fault. If she is doing wrong, she will have to pay for her negative actions. Why are you agonizing over them? It is like getting an upset stomach for someone else's indiscriminate eating. Don't burden yourself with another's flaws, and you will remain in an island of peace amidst a sea of turbulence. When you remain unaffected, you gain power. People will no longer mess with you. Bullies in school only pick on weak classmates to torment. They are afraid of the strong ones and leave them alone.

6

Open Your Mind to Greater Possibilities

However much you would like to believe in cause and effect, you often find people performing vicious acts and seemingly getting away with them. On the other hand, you see truly good people unnecessarily suffer for no fault of theirs. You wonder where the atonement happens and whether there is any justice at all in the world.

If you are the architect of your future, how do you find yourself in unpleasant situations? How is it that some people are in pathetic living conditions, malnourished and starving? Why are some differently abled, still others with genetic disorders, senior citizens suffering from painful ailments, and so on? Nobody would desire illness, poverty or deprivation. The parallelogram law of forces explains this phenomenon.

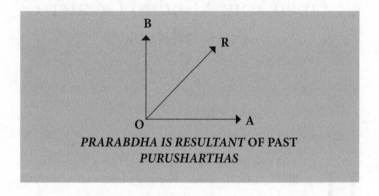

PRARABDHA IS RESULTANT OF PAST PURUSHARTHAS

Suppose there is an object O and there are two equal forces that act on it, one horizontally and the other vertically, the object will move at an angle of forty-five degrees, where no force is acting. This is the resultant of the two forces. If there are multiple forces acting on the object it will move in the direction of the resultant of all the forces. This is what physics tells us. Similarly, in the inner world, you entertain a variety of thoughts, desires and actions. What you face is the resultant of all these.

You have no idea where the resultant will take you. You carelessly think a negative thought here and a hurtful thought there, oblivious of the price you will have to pay for it. Have you noticed that you may have pretended to be ill to attract attention to yourself and ended up actually falling ill? The message is: be very careful about the kind of thoughts you think, emotions you feel and actions you perform. They may lead you to misery and suffering.

Be aware of your thoughts. Are you entertaining hateful thoughts? Are you negative in outlook? Are you constantly blaming others for the events in your life? Understand that it has nothing to do with others and that the source of frustration lies within you. As a human being, you are designed such that nothing in the world can disturb you except yourself. Look within. Identify the cause. Change your attitude. Attitude is the one thing that is entirely under your command. It is the one freedom that can never be taken away from you.

When you begin to see the beauty of life, ugliness fades away. Look at life with joy and enthusiasm, and sadness vanishes. Heaven and hell cannot coexist. It is up to you to choose.

Any change begins with your dissatisfaction with the present and a clear vision of a better future. When your mind opens to greater possibilities, the stage is set for change, revival and transformation. You understand a better quality of life awaits you. You see other people who have benefited from a positive outlook and behaviour.

You seek knowledge. You experiment with a new mindset. You make a concerted attempt to change the way you think. Then the results show, and you integrate the new approach in your life. You are a changed person.

At the beginning of the Bhagavad Gita, Arjuna was in a state of depression and despondency. He had laid down his bow and arrow and refused to fight. At the end of Krishna's message, which was about three hours long, Arjuna woke up from his stupor, fought the battle and won it!

The Three Rs

Life consists of three transactions. Stimuli from the world enter you through your organs of perception. You see, hear, smell, taste and touch various things. These stimuli are then transmitted to the sense centres in the mind. It is here that the perception gets registered. If you are engrossed in watching a match, even when a family member speaks to you, it does not register since the mind is preoccupied with the match.

At the level of the mind and intellect, there is a reaction between the stimulus that has entered and the desires in your mind. The mind is the realm of feelings and emotions, while the intellect is the domain of reason and discrimination. This reaction then expresses as a response back into the world as action. Thus, life consists of the three Rs – receipt of stimuli, reaction within and response into the world as action.

The stimulus being the same, the reaction varies in different people because of the nature of the mind. A person may be courteous and considerate towards you, but you may view it as hypocrisy and smooth talking because of your dislike for him. If your mother-in-law cooks a delicious meal, you cannot enjoy it if you are hateful towards her. In fact, whatever the mother-in-law does is viewed negatively by you. And you believe the problem is with her!

Similarly, when your boss gives valuable tips that will help you in your career, you reject them because of your dislike for him. And so on with all the people you have an aversion for, have a grudge against, or are vengeful towards. Your world becomes one of disgust, loathing and revulsion. The cause is within, but you see it out there. All your life you complain about people and situations outside, when just a slight shift in attitude will do the trick.

The first step is to bring your intellect, your rational aspect, into the picture. Separate the person from the qualities. Then you will see that the person is not bad. He is a good person with some bad traits. Just as you have some negativities, your family members have some irritating characteristics; they have their share of traits, some of which happen to annoy you.

View the dish the mother-in-law cooked without bringing her into the picture. Separate her from the food. Enjoy the food. Why pollute it with the hatred you have for her? View the tips the boss gives independent of your dislike for him. And so on. Life will become a little less depressing, a little happier for you.

Alan Turing was a brilliant mathematician from Cambridge and Princeton universities who worked for the British Government to decipher the secret code the Germans used during the Second World War. It is estimated that the efforts of Turing and his fellow code-breakers shortened the war by several years. Yet, he was difficult to get on with. His colleagues had to ignore his negativities and cooperate with him to obtain their goal for the country.

Everyone has shortcomings. You can either focus on them and create conflict and misery, or rise above them and identify with the positive traits. The choice is yours, one that will make a big difference to your life.

The next step is to examine why you dislike the person. It is possible that your aversion has nothing to do with the person. It may be your inflated ego that makes you view everyone as a competitor rather than partner. You may secretly admire the boss, but you view him as an obstacle in your career. The truth may be that he is actually trying to give you a promotion.

These unfounded aversions are the cause of tragedy in our lives. Duryodhana viewed the Pandavas as enemies, when they were actually his benefactors. Many times, Yuddhisthira and the other Pandavas saved him from sure death. But he was jealous of them and their goodness, strength and popularity. He chose to use all his resources to inflict pain and suffering on them. The Pandavas, in sharp contrast, ignored his viciousness and focused on their duty as brothers. In the end, Duryodhana only succeeded in destroying himself and brought about death and devastation all around. The Pandavas eventually gained the kingdom.

Shakespeare highlights this in his tragedies. Othello strangled his own wife to death on a mere suspicion planted by Iago, the villain of the piece. The real cause was his own inferiority complex, which led him to believe that she was unfaithful to him. Macbeth killed King Duncan, thinking that he would become king after him. King Duncan was actually his benefactor! Brutus assassinated Julius Caesar who truly loved him. And so are you killing perfectly wonderful relationships based on mere trifles, imagination and delusion.

Wake up to reality. See things as they are. Change your thoughts before you end up destroying yourself. Remember, hatred, revulsion and negativity will not do any harm to the people you despise. But it will wreak untold misery and hardship on you.

Cultivate powerful positive thoughts. Expose yourself to the wisdom of the masters. Change your attitude. Then the same world and the same stimuli will be viewed positively. Your reactions will be positive even when the stimulus is negative. In the movie *Life is Beautiful*, Guido converted life in a concentration camp into a happy experience for the sake of his four-year-old son. He spread cheer and laughter not only among the prisoners, but even the guards!

Buddha refused to get drawn into conflict with a man on the street who had abused him. When his disciples asked him why he did not react he said, 'He is free to say what he wants but it is my choice to receive what he says or return it. I chose not to take it so I was free. You people accepted it and hence the problem.'

As the mind changes, you no longer feel victimized by the world. You have the power to change your reactions. Your intellect then decides if the stimulus warrants a response. If so, you respond appropriately, powerfully and dynamically. Most times, foolishness, petty-mindedness and selfishness do not deserve a response. Ignore it and it will cease to bother you. If you react, you remain a victim of what the world throws at you. You have no control over the world, but you do have absolute and complete control over your own mind. 'Conquer the mind and you will conquer the world,' said Swami Vivekananda. You can experience it in your own life.

Bank of Karma

The loop of destiny and karma binds everyone. You remain entangled and imprisoned in it. The only way you can nullify it is by sustained, regular, intelligent movement, inward and upward. It is *purushartha* or free will that matters. It helps free you of the cycle of vasana-thought-desire-action-vasana. Irrespective of your past, if you perform constant, consistent, persistent, positive action, you wipe out the past negativity and sculpt a brilliant future.

Just as every drop of water saved helps conserve water, every thought, desire and action makes a difference in your life. It is with purushartha that an alcoholic becomes sober, a drug addict rehabilitates himself, an angry person gets even-tempered and a disorganized person learns discipline. Use this invaluable force within to change your life for the better. For this, you do not need a high IQ, more degrees or enhanced wealth. All it takes is a shift in outlook.

A man from a remote tribal village sees Person A withdraw cash at a bank and notices he still has a healthy balance in his account. He observes Person B deposit money but is still in the red. He thinks A is lucky and B is unlucky! He does not understand banking so he attributes it to fate. The truth is that Person A has deposited money in his bank account in the past while Person B already owes money to the bank. Irrespective of the balance in the account, if Person B, who is in debt, constantly puts in money, over a period of time he will be able to make good the deficit and have a surplus. This is simple. However, in the case of the Bank of Karma, there is no way of knowing what your past debits and credits are. You can only put in positive actions that will wipe out any debits that may be there and build a fantastic future for yourself.

BANK OF *KARMA* STATEMENT			
ACCOUNT A		**ACCOUNT B**	
BALANCE	+5	BALANCE	-3
WITHDRAWAL	-1	DEPOSITS	+1
	+4		-2
HENCE GAIN CREDIT, WIPE OUT DEFICIT			

Just make sure you shore up reserves in your karma account. Every thought, desire and action counts. Suddenly, when you have negated the effect of past negativities, you find good things happening in life. You get an unexpected inheritance from a relative, a huge bonus comes your way, or the value of a share you bought in the past mysteriously surges.

An honest police officer unexpectedly inherited a large apartment in an upmarket neighbourhood in Mumbai from his aunt. A bank clerk received a bonus that enabled him to pay for his daughter's wedding. A man in Bengaluru was seeking a loan to buy a home after his retirement. He suddenly realized that the value of the Infosys shares he had bought at par had skyrocketed and was enough to pay for his apartment. These are not coincidences. You get what you deserve, not what you desire – that's the Law of Karma.

By the same token, when bad things happen, do not get depressed or disheartened. Understand that you have sown the wrong seeds. All you have to do is correct the situation with positive thoughts.

It is not possible to know all your past actions, thoughts or feelings even in this lifetime. You have no idea what you may have done to a friend in primary school or how you may have hurt a colleague at work ten years back. And the memory of past lives is totally obliterated. Just ensure that every thought that you entertain, every emotion you feel and every act you perform is positive.

The change in circumstance may not happen immediately. But that it will happen is a given. Life takes on a magical turn. Inexplicable things happen in life. A maid who worked with a family in Dubai won a raffle ticket that paid millions. An Irish immigrant from a poor family struck gold in one business deal in Australia.

On the other hand, there are billionaires who go into severe depression, a couple loses an eighteen-year-old son in an accident, a lady is diagnosed with cancer in the prime of her career. People get knocked down with a series of mishaps and losses for which there seems to be no known cause. You may not be able to trace the cause, but that does not mean there is no cause. Attributing it to luck is irrational and dangerous.

Moment to moment, what you meet with is the resultant of all your past thoughts, desires and actions. But every individual thought goes towards influencing and determining the resultant. Hence, start with thought. Examine your emotions. Observe your actions. See if they are in line with the result you want to obtain. Will they get you success? Will you be happy? Will you grow to your potential? If not, change the cause. The effect will follow. It may take time to manifest. You do not have to worry about it.

Result of Action

While acting, there are two forces driving you. One is destiny, the effect from your past that pushes you in a particular direction. The other is free will that you may exert in another direction. You have a sweet tooth and eat chocolates and ice cream every day. Today, you may choose to abstain. The result may still be that you eat chocolate. But the choice you have made has influenced your destiny. A series of such choices will make you stop eating sweets!

You may be an ill-tempered person and give in to anger and temper tantrums. You may exercise free will today towards calmness, compassion and understanding. The force of destiny may prevail over the choice you have made now, and you may still scream and yell. But there is no taking away the fact that you have made an independent choice.

This impacts on your destiny. And constant choices made away from anger will eventually make you a gentle and good-natured person.

So, do not look for instant results and do not get discouraged when the transformation does not happen immediately. Just keep putting in positive efforts. Find fulfilment in the good choices you make. Success will be yours.

7

What Motivates Our Actions

There are two results that ensue from an action, thought, word or feeling. One is the immediate effect on your mind. You think a negative thought, and in that moment you are impoverished. You feel wretched. Entertain a loving thought, and immediately you are enriched by it. You feel happy. This is called *phala* or fruit of action. The other is the effect it has on your future life. It adds to your *samskaras* – leaves an imprint on your character, state of refinement or crudeness. This result manifests in the future. It takes a lot of effort and hard work to undo. So be careful in yielding to your base instincts.

It may be pleasant to yell at employees, your spouse or kids. But the consequences may be hard to bear.

Potency of Action

The potency of action depends on the level of awareness and the intention backing it. Where there is no awareness at all, there are no repercussions. A leopard or lion pounces on its prey and kills it. It does not cultivate murderous tendencies. Similarly, while walking along. you may inadvertently trample upon an insect. You do not have to pay for it. While acting, if you cause damage unintentionally, there will be consequences if you have been irresponsible and have not taken proper precautions.

In the Ramayana, Dasharatha wanted to show his prowess in archery. He shot an arrow in the direction of the sound of water, thinking it was an animal. It turned out he had killed a young boy, who had gone to the river to collect water for his blind parents. The story goes on to say the blind parents cursed him that he would also die in grief over his son. Much later, Dasharatha died in sorrow at having had to banish his beloved son Rama to fourteen years' exile.

Before you shoot, it is your obligation to ascertain who or what the target is. When you are behind the wheel of a car, it is your duty to make sure you do not cause hurt or loss of life to others.

A selfish action performed consciously, intending to hurt others, will boomerang on the perpetrator with interest. Not just simple interest or the interest that has to be paid for defaulting on credit card payments, but divine interest that is backbreaking. People are completely ignorant of this and recklessly speak harsh and hurtful words, cause financial loss to others or destroy them. Little do they know what havoc they are wreaking in their own lives. Even when they face the consequences, they blame someone or something in the environment rather than accept that it is their own past action catching up with them. All you have to do is understand that the Law of Karma is functioning.

People and circumstances are immaterial. What is important is that the law is playing out. Look within. Trace the cause. Change your attitude. Face the situation with courage and your future will change for the better. Otherwise, you will find the same problems recurring in some manner throughout life. This will not improve until you change the cause – your own action, attitude and thought.

Mediocrity to Excellence

The Bhagavad Gita highlights the value of unselfish action. In the third chapter entitled 'Karma Yoga', Krishna puts it dramatically and says in Verse 10:

> *sahayajnah prajah srshtva purovacha prajapatih*
> *anena prasavishyadhvamesha vo stvishtakamadhuk*
> Having created humankind in the beginning along with *yajna* (sacrifice), Prajapati the Creator said, 'By this may you prosper. Let this be the Kamadhenu of your endeavours.'

When the Creator made human beings, He blessed them with a special endowment, the gift of yajna, or sacrifice. Only human beings have the option of setting aside their personal interests and working for a higher cause. Yajna is the ability to work in a spirit of service and sacrifice for a noble ideal, the highest being Enlightenment. If you perform yajna, Kamadhenu, the heavenly cow blessed with the power to fulfil all your desires, will give you everything you want. But here Krishna says sacrifice becomes the Kamadhenu.

There are no shortcuts in life. There are no magic bullets. Accomplishments and greatness are a result of wholehearted, dedicated work towards a higher ideal. The higher the ideal and the harder you work, the luckier you get. It's not a coincidence. This is a truth that you can verify in your own life. The law of life is – give, you gain; grab, you lose.

Why do people suffer from the disease of more? Because they feel deprived and deficient. This is a state of mind that has nothing to do with your possessions. The wealthiest person in the world may feel deprived. A person in the ghettoes can feel abundant. Sudama, Krishna's childhood friend, lived all his life in poverty. Yet he never experienced want. He always felt abundant. Howard Hughes, once the richest man in the world, felt deprived and miserable.

The mind has the unique tendency to focus on the one little thing you do not have and to make you miserable over it. The intellect has the ability to look at all the things you have and enjoy them. The mind and intellect make your inner personality. The mind is the realm of feelings, emotions and impulses. It is the irrational aspect in you. The intellect is the domain of discrimination, analysis and judgement – your rational component.

When you are aware of all that you have received in life, for free and in abundance, you develop the irresistible desire to give, contribute, share your good fortune with others. You get into giving mode, away from the urge to grab.

The Power of Love

The next potent karma is the feeling of loving kindness towards all beings – universal love. The Bhagavad Gita gives thirty-five qualities of a devotee of God, of which the very first is – one who hates no being. It is no use declaring love for an unknown, unseen God, when you feel hatred towards people you see, know and interact with. Yet we live in a world where human beings are causing unimaginable pain and suffering to millions of people across the world. Animals are subject to untold misery from the day they are born till they are mercilessly slaughtered in meat farms. How can you expect any degree of peace or happiness?

Start with the person you dislike the most. Why do you hate him? You believe it is because the person has certain disgusting qualities. But the person has other good qualities too. In the Ramayana, Rama told Lakshmana to learn administration and other royal duties from Ravana, who was a demon and had done many evil things. You also have negativities. What gives you the right to criticize and hate others?

When you set aside your prejudice and view others objectively, you see their good qualities too. You understand how difficult it is to change your faults. Then how can you expect a person, who may not be aware of his shortcomings, to change? Accept him for what he is. Love him as he is. This is a true *bhakta*, a devotee of God.

Be grateful for all that you have received in life, unasked for, unknown and unacknowledged. You do not know who has blessed you, but you know that you have been bestowed innumerable blessings. You will develop the universal feeling of love towards all beings.

Impermanence of World

The insight into the impermanence of the world is profound. It deconditions you and opens up the pathway to liberation, wisdom and Enlightenment. Actions directed towards Enlightenment are the most potent. Then even the forces of nature bow to you in deference.

Prahlada was a young boy, who was a devotee of Lord Vishnu. His father, Hiranyakashyapu, was king of the Demons. He was incensed with Prahlada for not owing allegiance to him and plotted to kill him. Fire could not burn him, the venom of snakes was ineffective when used against him, and elephants could not trample upon him. In the end, Prahlada was saved by Narasimha – the frightening half-lion, half-man form of Vishnu – who killed Hiranyakashyapu. Prahlada then became the king of the demons and all his subjects, who were evil, transformed into noble people.

When you become acutely aware of the fragility and impermanence of the world, you develop the right value for it. The right value is zero. Sri Ramakrishna said the value of the world and everything in it is zero. Accumulate seven zeroes, the total value is still zero. Add a one before the zeroes and there is tremendous value addition. It becomes ten million! The one is Spirit, or Atman. Atman makes the difference. Without Atman, the best that the world has to offer becomes insipid and boring, just as the best car in the world becomes junk without fuel. In a place without electricity, the most expensive electrical gadget is scrap. Similarly, the most exquisite life becomes useless without the thought of the higher realities.

In the end, it is the thought backing the action, the intention behind the action, which makes the difference. Not the action per se. Perform action with your heart and soul, with utmost dedication, deep devotion and acute awareness. The result will be astounding.

SECTION III

The Cycle of Life

8

Reincarnation

What happens after death and what brings about birth? This is a mystery that baffles the human mind. The word 'reincarnation' is derived from Latin and literally means 'to take on flesh again'. The Sanskrit word is *punarjanma*, birth again. What exactly is reincarnation? It means you leave one body and go into another. This is for the sole purpose of self-development and spiritual growth.

Tragically, all we do is increase the load of desires, life after life, and go further downhill. This doctrine is the central tenet of Indian philosophy. Reincarnation implies that the person remains essentially the same while occupying a new body, in a different environment.

Ancient Indian seers, men and women of Enlightenment, analysed the data and arrived at an irrefutable, scientific conclusion. They acknowledged that their findings cannot be proven as there is complete obliteration of memory at death and you are born with a clean slate. This is a blessing and enables you to start afresh instead of being weighed down by past memories. Remembering the problems of one lifetime is burdensome enough. What would happen if we remembered the challenges of past lives? Hence, they called it the *theory* of reincarnation and not *law*. This does not change the validity of their findings.

Just as in a court of law there are judgements passed entirely on circumstantial evidence, ancient Indian sages made their conclusions based on scientific data. They found that the universe functions on cause and effect. Every cause has an effect and for every effect there is a cause. The basis of their findings is similar to the first law of thermodynamics, which states that energy can neither be created or destroyed. It can only be transferred from one form to another.

They examined the abrupt loss of energy, desires, aspirations and goals at death and connected them with the sudden appearance of distinct characteristics, qualities and desires at birth. In other words, at death, each person has latent desires and thoughts that seem to vanish into nothing. These are causes for which there are no known effects. On the other hand, each infant is born with a distinct personality, likes, dislikes and traits. These too are effects with no known causes. All they did was to connect the unknown effects at death with the unknown causes at birth. Then the pieces of the jigsaw puzzle fell in place.

Modern psychiatry has accommodated the theory of reincarnation and some therapists have successfully used past-life regression to solve deep psychiatric issues that were plaguing patients. Belief in reincarnation is central to many major religions like Hinduism, Buddhism, Jainism and Sikhism. Gilgul is the concept of reincarnation in Kabbalistic Judaism.

According to data released by the Pew Forum on Religion and Public Life (2009 survey), not only do a quarter of Americans believe in reincarnation, but

24 per cent of American Christians also expressed a belief in reincarnation.

An article in *Nordic Psychology* says that for the combined fifteen countries of western Europe, the percentage of believers in life after death is 59 per cent. The belief in reincarnation is highest in Switzerland – 36 per cent.

To understand what happens after death, let us take a look at what happens during our lifetime. Moment to moment, experience to experience, you move, driven by desire. Why do you move out of your home in the morning? Because desire propels you – to school, your place of work, shopping mall or hospital. Where do you go next? Wherever your next predominant desire takes you. From the time you wake up till the time you go to sleep, you move motivated by desire. Desire is the fuel that propels motion. This goes on from birth to death.

You go to a mall with a list of things you want to buy. At the mall you enter a shoe store because you want to buy shoes. You remain there until the desire is fulfilled and you buy the shoes you wanted. You move to the next item on your desire list – perfume.

Then you move to the clothes section. And so on until you exit the mall when your list has been exhausted and you have fulfilled the desires that brought you to the mall.

Similarly, you enter the mall of life because you have the fuel of desires. During your lifetime you move from experience to experience, from one place to another driven by desire. You enter the shopping mall with only a few desires – for shoes, perfume and clothes. The other desires remain dormant. These are many more and they surface at different times in your life. Similarly, you are born in this life with a small bundle of desires that are strong, pushing for fulfilment. These are called *prarabdha vasanas*, which are ripe to be experienced in this lifetime.

During your lifetime, the one thing you are assured of is that the prarabdha vasanas will be fulfilled, irrespective of what you do or not do. The total number of desires you have is called *sanchita vasanas*. Of these, the prarabdha vasanas are only a few. All other beings live out their prarabdha vasanas but have no access to their sanchita vasanas, the total desires. Only human beings have the privilege of tapping into the sanchita. You can add to them, subtract from them, upgrade or downgrade them. By this you can change your life. You can even eliminate them completely and reach the exalted state of Enlightenment!

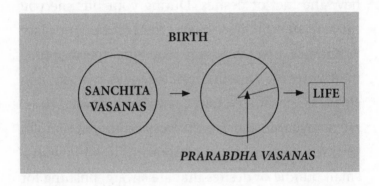

When and why does death take place? Death is the movement of the vasanas, mind and intellect from one body to another. When death occurs, the body is there. Spirit, the God-Principle, is also present as It is all-pervading and cannot move. What is missing is the vasanas, which are the blueprint or philosophical code of your personality and the mind and intellect, which together form your inner personality. Why do they move?

Once the bundle of prarabdha vasanas, which have determined this life, are fulfilled, the next bunch of strong vasanas or desires that are clamouring for expression, start operating. These are usually very different from the earlier lot of vasanas. So there is a disconnect between these desires and the present body and environment. The next lot of prarabdha vasanas have no scope for fulfilment. There is a cry for change. Nature gives you a wonderful opportunity to move on to another body and circumstance that are best suited for the fulfilment of the next bundle of prarabdha vasanas.

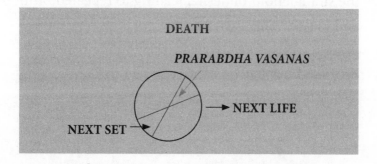

During life, the default setting provided by Nature is that the prarabdha vasanas will get fulfilled. Death cannot happen unless these vasanas are exhausted.

Once the prarabdha vasanas are exhausted, death has to take place. Nothing can prevent it. This explains how, in a car accident, only one person dies while the others escape with minor scratches. On the other hand, in Kentucky, a child miraculously survived a plane crash in which everyone else perished.

This process goes on as long as you have the fuel of desires. We are helplessly caught in the sequence of birth and death, driven by desire. Only when you have exhausted all the sanchita vasanas is there freedom from the incessant, helpless cycle of change. A rare one has the vision of freedom from the stranglehold of desire, leading to repeated birth and death. The vast majority of humans have a limited, constricted, view of life and are content to be tossed by the constant cycle of birth and death. As Adi Shankaracharya says in *Bhaja Govindam*, his original composition on life:

Punarapi jananam punarapi maranam
Punarapi janani jathare shayanam
Iha samsare bahudustare
Krpayapare pahi murare

Birth, death and sleeping in the mother's womb over and over again – this *samsara* (world) is unfathomable and difficult to cross.
O Murari (Krishna), protect me by your grace.

Every religion speaks of the concept of heaven and hell. How does this fit into the theory of reincarnation? It is said that rebirth does not take place immediately after death. For some time, the inner personality experiences dream and deep sleep, exactly the way we do during life.

What kind of dreams will you have? If you have led a negative life of selfishness, performing desire-driven vicious actions, you will go through nightmares. This is referred to as hell. If you have performed noble, unselfish actions, you will have happy, pleasant dreams, which are heavenly. After this, you will take birth in a new body.

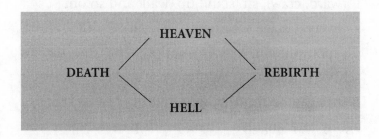

During each lifetime, while you have the option of reducing and eliminating all your vasanas – and the universe is designed just right to facilitate this process – all that you do is subtract a few, add a few more and end up with a greater number of vasanas than you were born with. Thus, you condemn yourself to many more lives in this mortal, grief-stricken world. The rare ones, with the vision of freedom from these traumatic changes, forge a different path. They are the ones who truly succeed and attain their purpose and mission in life.

The Bhagavad Gita speaks of the insight into the pain and suffering of birth, growth, disease, decay and death. These changes make the life of every living being. There is pain at every stage. An infant comes into the world wailing. It cannot be a pleasant experience. Thereafter, every change is harrowing. The infant struggles to turn over on its stomach, go forward, crawl, sit, stand up, walk and so on.

Every stage brings its share of effort, disappointment and frustration. The first day of school is traumatic. Adolescence and the changes it brings can be mortifying. Adult life has its share of agony and anguish. Then youth passes before you know it and the rest of your life is only downhill. Old age brings with it illness, loneliness and the sinking feeling of not being wanted. The wise one who sees this opts out of the cycle of birth and death and yearns for *moksha*, or freedom – a life without the ups and downs of human existence.

9

The Path of Non-Return

King Uttanapada had two wives – Suruchi and Suniti. One day, when Dhruva, son of Suniti, was sitting on his father's lap, the jealous Suruchi threw him away and placed her own son on the king's lap. The heartbroken Dhruva went weeping to his mother and told her about the incident. In her wisdom, Suniti made no reference to the stepmother. Instead, she told Dhruva that life is a mix of good and bad. Sometimes happy incidents happen, at other times sorrow strikes. Dhruva asked her, 'Where can I find only happiness?' She said only when you reach God will you be truly happy and no sorrow will come to you. He then asked, 'Where is God?' She said God was inside, in the core of every person.

The five-year-old Dhruva set off to find God. When he was in deep meditation, Lord Vishnu, pleased with his effort, appeared before him and said, 'Dhruva, you wanted me. Here I am. Open your eyes!' Dhruva refused, saying, 'My mother told me you were inside me. If you are God meet me inside!' This was the final test Dhruva was put to, and instantly he realized God. Till this day, the pole star is named after Dhruva. Dhruva means constant, immovable, fixed.

When you begin to understand the severe strictures on happiness that the world imposes, you are no longer content with life as you know it. You look for something beyond. This is where the spiritual journey begins.

Siddhartha Gautama was born into an affluent, royal family. It was predicted that he would become either a great king or a spiritual leader. His father showered him with the best the world could provide and tried to prevent Siddhartha from seeing the sorrowful side of life. He surrounded him with every kind of pleasure one could conceive. Siddhartha had a beautiful, good wife and a charming son.

Suddenly, at the age of twenty-nine, he was exposed to impermanence and suffering. He saw a diseased person, an old man, a corpse and, finally, a monk. He realized that the perfection he had been seeking outside was within him and that he had to find it. Thus began his spiritual quest that culminated in his transformation to the Buddha. Buddha literally means to be awakened. India has been home to countless such people who changed the direction of their pursuit and reached Enlightenment. They then showed the way to the ignorant masses and inspired them to follow suit.

In the poem 'The Rime of the Ancient Mariner' Samuel Coleridge recounts the experiences of a sailor who has returned from a long voyage. The mariner stops one of three men who are on their way to a wedding ceremony and begins to narrate his story. The wedding guest's reaction turns from bemusement to impatience to fear to fascination as the mariner's story progresses. Eventually, he turns away from the wedding and follows the Mariner.

The Mariner represents an enlightened person who has just emerged from the voyage of life and is eager to pass on the knowledge to people. The three wedding guests are the three types of people – *sattvika*, *rajasika* and *tamasika* – the pure, the passionate and the apathetic. We all have a worldly agenda, something that keeps us engaged and attached to the world. An enlightened Master connects with the sattvika one, you, and begins his narration. The other two are zoned out. Initially, you are confused; you get irritated because your worldly plan has been upset. But then, there is something about the Master and the sparkle in his eye that fascinates you. You listen eagerly and in the end, you turn away from materialistic pursuits to follow the spiritual path. This is beautifully portrayed by Coleridge:

It is an ancient Mariner,
And he stoppeth one of three.
'By thy long grey beard and glittering eye,
Now wherefore stopp'st thou me?' ...

He holds him with his glittering eye—
The Wedding-Guest stood still,

And listens like a three years' child:
The Mariner hath his will.

The Wedding-Guest sat on a stone:
He cannot choose but hear;
And thus spake on that ancient man,
The bright-eyed Mariner.

Life presents a choice of two paths – the path of return and the path of non-return. Those who live within the scope of desire and perform only desire-driven actions have to return as they have the driving force of desire that needs to be exhausted. A person who has performed negative, selfish actions, cultivates negative desires, the result of which condemns him to hell before he is reborn. Even during his lifetime, he experiences a hellish existence of stress, trauma and sorrow. One who has positive desires and performs dedicated, unselfish actions goes to heaven and enjoys pleasures many times those on earth, but has to return because of desires. Even while he is alive, his life is one of joy, happiness and fulfilment.

PATH OF RETURN

HELL
DESIRE-RIDDEN NEGATIVE ACTIONS

HEAVEN
DESIRE-RIDDEN POSITIVE ACTIONS

Extraordinary people who understand the futility of worldly existence and the burden it imposes have the vision of the beyond. They understand that it is desire that keeps them confined and stunted. They choose *moksha*, or freedom, and opt out of the gambit of desire. They perform selfless actions directed towards Realization or Enlightenment. They follow the spiritual path aimed at obliterating desire.

Along the way, a few aspirants slip into attachment and desire if the intellect is not alert and vigilant. They perform great service to the world, but stray into desire-driven action. Though noble, this delays their progress to Enlightenment. After death, they are transported to Brahmaloka, a superior quality of heaven where the enjoyment is 4.32 billion times the best that the world has to offer. After living there for a long period of time when their *punya*, or effect of their good karma, is exhausted they finally reach Enlightenment. This is called *krama mukti*, or realization in stages.

PATH OF NO RETURN

KRAMA MUKTI
DESIRE-RIDDEN POSITIVE & OBLIGATORY ACTION

KAIVALYA MUKTI
ONLY OBLIGATORY ACTION

The rare wise person is ever alert and keeps the mind free from any entanglement in the world. He exercises extreme caution and keeps his thought anchored in the goal at all times. Such a person goes straight to Enlightenment while living in the body. This is called *kaivalya mukti*, or direct liberation.

Say, you have to go to New York for an important meeting and the travel agent offers you a choice: you can either take a flight that offers a halt in Dubai with loads of freebies, or a non-stop direct flight to New York. Which one would you take? You would opt for the non-stop flight as your focus is on the meeting in New York. Similarly, what is the lure of heavenly joys to a person who is focused on the Infinite?

One such person was the teenage boy Nachiketa in the Kathopanishad. He was the son of the sage Vajashravas. Once, Vajasharavas performed a yajna, sacrificial ritual, at which one is supposed to donate all of one's possessions. Nachiketa noticed that his father was only giving old cows that had stopped yielding milk. To save him from the terrible fate that would befall him, Nachiketa asked him whom he would give his son to. The father did not reply but when Nachiketa persisted and asked him the third time, he flew into a rage and said, 'I will give you to Yama!' Yama is the god of death.

Unhesitatingly, Nachiketa went to Yama but had to wait for three days as Yama was away. When Yama returned, he offered Nachiketa three boons to compensate for the three days he was kept waiting. Nachiketa went about it systematically. His first obligation was to the immediate family so he asked for his father to regain his composure as he was very stressed when Nachiketa decided to go to Yama. Yama immediately granted his wish. The next obligation was to the world. Nachiketa asked Yama to teach him the art of doing service to the world. Yama obliged, and Nachiketa did it so wholeheartedly and perfectly that Yama gave him a necklace of precious gems and said that from then on the sacrifice would be named after him. The third duty is towards yourself and Nachiketa asked for Enlightenment, *Brahma Vidya*, knowledge of Brahman, God. Now, Yama hesitated as he wanted to make sure the young man was prepared for it and knew what he was asking for. So he offered him instead heavenly cows that represented the wealth of the heavens!

Nachiketa was not interested and turned the other way. It so happened that beautiful damsels were dancing in the direction of his gaze. Yama thought if wealth does not tempt the young man maybe this would so he said, 'You can have them too!' This is when Nachiketa made the famous statement, '*Tavaiva vahastava nritya gite* (you keep your song and dance). Teach me Brahma Vidya.' Yama was pleased and gave him the most invaluable knowledge that took Nachiketa from a life of confinement and limitation to that state of infinite happiness, free from the shackles of worldly existence.

So, you have to decide which of the paths you want to follow. If you want to be on the non-stop treadmill of desire, having to run faster and faster for rewards that mean less each time, the wise masters say go ahead and enjoy the world. But beware of desire. Trying to fulfil desire by providing it with the object of desire is like attempting to put out fire by adding fuel to it! If you have chased after a desire and finally fulfilled it, only to feel cheated at the end of it all, you need to think afresh. You feel like a donkey that has a carrot dangling at the end of a cart. You keep running towards it. However fast you run, the happiness you seek is still out of reach and will always be beyond your grasp. Because you are looking for it in the wrong place.

Happiness

Everyone in the world is chasing after happiness. Nobody seems to know where it is. We all suffer from the JATC syndrome: happiness seems to be Just Around The Corner! Happiness is not just the birthright of every individual but it is your duty. Your primary obligation in life is to be cheerful, full of enthusiasm, exhilaration and excitement. We chase after desire. When the desire is fulfilled, the agitation of the mind ceases, at least for a while. So you believe that happiness lies out there in the object. Thus we are caught in the vortex of the three Es – Entertainment, Excitement and Exhaustion. You look forward to a vacation, you get excited over it, and after the vacation, you are so exhausted you need another weekend to recover from it.

Happiness is within you. Yet everyone is looking for it outside. Once, a businessman was carrying a lot of cash from one city to another by train. A thief got wind of it and boarded the same compartment with the idea of stealing the cash. It was an overnight journey. The businessman had his dinner in a relaxed manner while chatting with the thief. He then went to the washroom and took his time there. The moment the businessman left, the thief got busy looking for the cash. He looked everywhere but could not find it. The businessman returned and fell asleep. The thief was puzzled about the cash and could not sleep a wink. The next morning he could not contain himself. He confessed to the businessman that he had boarded the train only to steal his cash but could not find it. The businessman leaned across and pulled out the cash from under the thief's pillow!

If happiness were in the object, the same item should give equal joy to all. This does not happen. The object being the same, one person finds immense happiness in it while another finds it abhorrent. A smoker comes out of an airport terminal and lights up a cigarette. He is delighted. Another finds the same smoke disgusting and suffocating.

As long as a desire remains unfulfilled, you are unhappy. The moment you gain the object of desire, you are happy, at least for the moment. Hence, you believe it is the object that makes you happy. The truth is that as long as the desire remains unfulfilled, the mind is agitated. When the desire is fulfilled the mind is at peace. The fundamental error in believing that happiness lies out there needs to be examined.

Dan Gilbert, professor of psychology at Harvard University, says there are two kinds of happiness – natural and synthetic. Natural happiness comes when you fulfil a desire. You have a desire for food.

You eat and you are happy. This is experienced by all other living beings too. Human beings have the additional capacity to manufacture the very commodity they are seeking out there in the world. You can synthesize happiness. In other words, you have the capacity to be happy whether or not you gain the object of your desire. You have a psychological immune system that can manufacture the very thing you are seeking outside.

When a dog gets a bone, it is happy. If the dog is denied a bone, it cannot be happy. As a human, you can be happy even when you do not get the bone. This capability is not known and therefore not exercised. Ancient Indians focused on this very gift as there is no guarantee that the world will provide you with objects of desire. Besides, you become hopelessly dependent on the world.

As long as your attention is outward, looking to the world for fulfilment, you will always be agitated and unhappy. There will be an ever-widening gap between your desires and the objects you obtain. Even if you do gain everything, the law of diminishing returns kicks in. The more you indulge, the less you enjoy. The greatest enjoyment lies in the first contact with an object. Every subsequent contact reduces the joy content. So you have more of it to regain the enjoyment.

Take the case of a person who has his first alcoholic drink. It gives him a thrill. So he has a drink every day. Soon, it stops yielding joy. So he has two drinks a day and regains the joy. Over time, even this loses its thrill, so he goes on increasing his intake till he could be consuming a great deal, with zero enjoyment! Yet he needs to continue drinking because not having it gives him sorrow. He is completely neutralized to alcohol. When he consumes it, he gets no particular enjoyment, but when he is denied it, he is miserable.

This happens to all of us. The more affluent you are, the greater is the affliction. You get neutralized to one object so you move to another one. Initially, you are excited but the honeymoon is soon over. You move to something else. And something else … Until you are neutralized to almost all objects! When you have the good things of life, you get no pleasure. When you do not have any of those objects, you get displeasure. You have reached a stalemate. You need to work hard to maintain a high standard of living, all for nothing. No benefit. You alternate between no joy and displeasure. This is when depression sets in.

Turn inward, and you will find happiness. You are at peace with yourself. You discover a happiness that remains even when you do not obtain the object of desire. In fact, it has no connection with the object of desire. You finally understand the devastating effects of desire. You are now convinced that the very thing you were cultivating, nourishing, nurturing and fanning is your greatest enemy.

10

Desire Is the Devil

Krishna, in the Bhagavad Gita, uses four words to describe desire, all of which mean enemy – *vairin, nitya vairin, paripanthin* and *shatru*. And desire is the very thing you are befriending! You may have observed that as long as you craved for a thing, you did not get it. When you got over the obsession and moved on, you got it. Whether it was a particular toy you wanted in childhood or the dream dress you craved for as a teenager, it is desire that stands between you and the object of desire.

Unfulfilled desire causes unhappiness. Stress is defined as mental agitation caused by unfulfilled desire. You are free to cultivate desire. But the world is not obliged to satisfy it. The more unrealistic the desire you entertain, the greater is the sorrow you experience.

And desire keeps you stunted. Your vision gets obstructed and all your talent and ability lie untapped, unknown, unsuspected!

Desire and Its Mutations

Desire is described as the devil in every religion. Hinduism refers to desire as Asura, Christianity says it is Satan, Islam calls it Shaitan, and in Buddhism it is Mara.

Whether fulfilled or frustrated, desire causes agitation and unrest in the mind. Let us see what desire does in our system. Desire is like a virus or bacterium. One virus seems innocuous. What is its strength compared to the power and sophistication of a human being? Yet, once it gets into you, it renders your immune system ineffective, multiplies fast and does not let go until it has destroyed you.

In the second chapter of the Bhagavad Gita, Krishna describes the stairway to destruction. It begins with a thought, just one thought. A thought here and a like there seem harmless. It is pleasant to think of a Tesla car or a holiday to an exotic location, so you dwell on it. Before long, it becomes a stream of thoughts going from you to the object. This is called attachment. You have become attached to the concept of having the object. You further invest in the thought and it becomes a strong desire to obtain the object. Now you are stuck. You have to get it. You then go off at a tangent, set aside your life goals and run after the object. This could have dangerous implications.

An athlete who has gone to San Francisco for an international tournament sees a brand new seven-seater Tesla car. The athlete is fond of cars and enjoys rides in the Tesla. She thinks of the car. She gets attached to the idea of buying a Tesla for herself and develops a desire for it. Thereafter, instead of focusing on her events and performance she is now planning on importing the car into India, trying to arrange for the finances, and so on. In the end, she gets so caught up with the car that she performs badly at her events and loses her career. She also fails to get the car.

If the desire is fulfilled, you are happy for a while, but then you want more. The desire morphs into greed. A businessman starts with modest goals. Once he gets a taste of success, he wants more. The desire is fulfilled further, and he gets deluded with the success. He thinks he can buy everything with his money. Sadly, the only thing that wealth can get you is sense objects. With wealth, you cannot buy love and you certainly cannot get knowledge. You earn even more wealth and you reach the very top. But then you are consumed with fear: fear of losing the money, fear that the economy will crash, the stock market will go down, or that your son-in-law will take it away!

There will always be someone who has more than you. One may be better-looking than you, another more popular than you, a third more talented. You are envious of those who have more. And you are arrogant towards those you perceive as being less endowed than you.

All this creates a lot of mental agitation and stress. You are unable to enjoy life. You suffer from insomnia. The stress affects both the body and the mind. It manifests as a variety of physical ailments.

Hypertension, heart attacks, strokes and other diseases have been attributed to stress. Desire attacks the mind too. You go into depression. The fact that an anti-depressant is the highest-selling drug in the United States speaks of the devastation that desire has caused.

Yet the world over, people are promoting desire, encouraging it, nurturing and nourishing it. When the ancient masters warn against the ill effects of desire, we dismiss their advice because we believe they are telling us to keep away from objects of desire. This is the one misunderstanding that has caused untold suffering in the world. When they ask us to rise above desire, they are not telling us to give up objects of desire. In fact, they are prescribing ways of obtaining more of the world. The mantra is – acquire, possess and enjoy as much of the world as you can. But never desire it.

It is desire that is the devil, not the world. As long as you desire anything, you remain a slave to it. You are subservient to it and wholly dependent on it. Entertain a higher desire. You will be freed from the lower desire. The object of desire will come to you. This happens because you develop merit. The world amply rewards a person of accomplishment in any field of endeavour.

Whether you are a sportsperson, musician, or architect, concentrate on improving your performance. Do everything that will enhance your skills and abilities. Your earnings will automatically go up. If you just think of money, you will become mediocre and money will elude you. So, set aside desire and focus on developing excellence.

The law of life is that you get what you deserve, not what you desire. Focus on deserving, never on desiring. The good things of life come to an outstanding sportsperson, scientist or business executive, who has gained merit. We only see the laurels and accolades, luxury cars, fame and fortune that people enjoy. We do not see the hard work that brought them all of this.

Kobe Bryant, the iconic basketball player who tragically died in a helicopter crash in January 2020, worked harder and earlier than even the NBA's best players. From marathon shooting sessions to a relentless desire to improve himself and refusing to eat the junk food he loved, Kobe was driven to be the best. He was always the first player in the gym, even when he was hurt. In high school, he would show up for practice at 5.00 a.m. and leave at 7.00 a.m. Later, his workout began at 4.15 a.m. Even when he was fit, he went on a punishing diet to knock off 16 pounds for the 2012 Olympics.

Look at the hard work, sacrifice and effort that makes for success. Get inspired by achievers who have gone through the struggle and enjoyed the exertion. Emulate them. Success will automatically come to you. There are no shortcuts in life. No instant riches.

Similarly, there is a price to be paid for happiness. You must work at deserving happiness, contentment and joy. It doesn't just come down on you one fine day. This is even more so with spiritual evolution. It takes effort of a different kind, one that is more arduous but far more enriching and fulfilling. The by-products of spiritual development are immense prosperity and happiness. So go for spiritual growth. The wealth of the world will be at your command. And you will be happy, irrespective of what happens around you.

SECTION IV

The Way Out

11

Rise Above Desire

What is the solution? What is to be done with desire? The way out is to first scan the desires with the intellect. Let the intellect examine the desires and decide which ones to fulfil and which ones to delete. The intellect should guide, supervise and direct desires. Thus, desire takes on the less virulent form of aim, ambition and aspiration – just as the same virus that is harmful becomes a vaccine when attenuated.

Let us take a look at what desire does. It stands in the way of obtaining the object of desire. As long as you are obsessed with a desire, the object of desire eludes your grasp. It takes the form of craving, hankering, pining for the object. You then have a limited view of life, the mind is agitated, you cannot think clearly and action is flawed.

Look back in your life. Whenever you desperately wanted a toy, dress or gadget, you were denied it. Then, you moved on and suddenly the very thing you were craving for came to you! So chase after a desire and the object of desire slips away. Rise above desire and the object of desire comes to you. By all means, have objects of desire. Possess and enjoy what the world has to offer. But never desire anything.

Desire comes in the way of enjoyment. Only a person not obsessed with things can enjoy them. If you are infatuated with something, you cannot enjoy it. An alcoholic does not enjoy liquor. Only a person not fixated on liquor enjoys a drink. It is the same with food. A glutton only consumes large quantities of food. He does not enjoy it. One who is not excessively attached to food relishes it.

Desire makes you unhappy. Unfulfilled desire causes mental agitation and stress. The stress further comes in the way of enjoyment. And desire makes you stunted and handicapped. You cannot achieve greatness with a small mind. Your vision needs to expand beyond just the thought of 'I, me and myself'.

What is the source of desire? How is a desire born? Desire comes where there is a void. When the stomach is empty, thoughts go towards food. When you have already eaten, the mind will not entertain the thought of food. So emptiness is the precursor to desire. Look within. From the moment you wake up till the time you go to sleep, from birth to death, all humans are consumed by a feeling of emptiness and unfulfilment. As physics says, 'Nature abhors vacuum.' So thoughts arise in your mind, which go out to the world to obtain objects and beings to fill the void.

You invest in one thought, and the thicker stream of thought is called desire. In life, you have fulfilled many desires. Has the feeling of emptiness gone? Has it even reduced? No. Have you wondered why the emptiness does not go in spite of fulfilling so many desires? The Bhagavad Gita explains this phenomenon. It says that even as you feel this gnawing sense of emptiness, you are actually full. Completely and totally fulfilled. But for some inexplicable reason, you do not know that you are full.

This ignorance of your fullness makes you a fool. So, all of humanity is barking up the wrong tree! You do not need objects of desire. All you need is knowledge of your fullness. Then desire will automatically vanish. You will attain the ultimate purpose of your life – total and complete happiness. So, continue fulfilling desires. But spend a little time gaining knowledge of your fullness.

The Bhagavad Gita prescribes a scientific method to deal with desire. We call it VOS, the Vedanta Operating Systems, a highly efficient way of purifying your personality of desires. It enables you to reduce the number of desires with the Path of Action, upgrade the quality of desires with the Path of Devotion and change the direction of desires with the Path of Knowledge.

12

Path of Action

To begin with, examine what motivates you to act. Do you feel deprived? Do you work to acquire more of the world? Or do you feel blessed and want to share your good fortune with others? When you look at the things you do not have, you do the least possible, you constantly blame others, you have a pessimistic view of life, and you only look for personal profit and pleasure. Become aware of the abundance you have been blessed with. Then you will be jumping out of bed every day with a child's excitement. You will develop the urge to give, to share your good fortune with others less privileged.

You will be enthusiastic, go beyond the call of duty, become creative.

Move from the attitude of taking, grabbing, aggrandizing to that of giving, sharing, contributing. From profiteering to offering, from merely enriching yourself to adding value to others. The way to gain is by giving. Physics validates this principle. An object is red in colour because it absorbs all other colours except red. Strangely, the other six colours it retains, it loses. The only colour it gives, it has! So is it with us. Give a little, you gain a little. Give more, you receive more. Give all, you get all.

The Rig Veda says, 'Money is like manure. Hoard it in one place, it pollutes the air. Spread it over fields and you get a bumper harvest!' You do not have to give anything. Just think of giving and that moment you are enriched. By the same token, plan on grabbing and you are instantly impoverished.

The attitude of giving pays rich dividend even in the field of business, where the objective is profit. CVS has a sign at its corporate headquarters that reads, 'Helping people on their path to better health'. Their executives see their company as having a purpose beyond just making money. The one thing they could not come to terms with is how they could sell cigarettes if the health of their customers was at the heart of their business. In February 2014, CVS took a decision to stop selling tobacco-related products in all their 7,800 outlets. This decision would cost them over 2 billion dollars per year in revenue lost.

Initially, the stock price went down and Wall Street analysts were not too pleased. But a year and a half later, the stock price went to almost double of what it had been before they made the momentous decision. Ethical companies decided to partner with them, and they more than made up for the loss incurred by not selling cigarettes.

It takes courage to adopt a standard of ethics higher than the law. How can you find the courage to take a stand and change your mindset? You can wait for a traumatic experience to shake you out of your slumber and force you to change. This is how most people change. Something acts as a trigger – tragedy, circumstances or divine intervention – to see things differently.

In the movie *Ultimate Gift*, the spoilt grandson of a billionaire, who has never thought of anyone other than himself, is now pushed by the grandfather's will to see another aspect of life. He sees a little girl suffering from cancer and her mother struggling to find the resources to take care of her. His attitude changes. He decides to adopt a higher cause and pledges the 100 million dollars he has to form a trust for the welfare of kids suffering from cancer. That moment, he inherits the entire fortune of his grandfather!

Alternatively, you can find a just cause that inspires you. Then you surround yourself with likeminded people and watch your dream come alive before your eyes. In 2013, the two founders of the company 'Beats', Andre Young, popularly known as Dr Dre, and Jimmy Iovine, went to Steve Jobs whom they hugely admired. They asked him how they could get more people like Jobs, who was an amazing combination of aesthetics, technology and a superb business head. Steve Jobs told them to start a course that combined the three streams. They donated thirty-five million dollars each to the University of Southern California to establish the Academy for Arts, Technology and the Business of

Innovation. A year later, Apple acquired Beats and each of them got 1.5 billion dollars!

Mediocre people have a myopic vision of profit and pleasure for themselves. They cannot see anything beyond I, me and myself. They are driven by the desire for personal enhancement and enjoyment. They achieve limited ends. They are unhappy, as all selfish people are miserable. And they remain stunted all their lives. Great leaders have a vision, a goal, an ideal beyond their selfish, self-centred interests. They embrace a higher cause, an unselfish purpose. They are the ones who achieve success. They are happy irrespective of what the world offers them. And they grow into towering personalities.

Identify your *svadharma*, your talent, nature, the special gift you were born with. Recognize your passion and invest your energies in that field. Most people choose vocations in which they think they will make money. How can you succeed in a field alien to your nature, in which you have no interest or ability? Don Bradman may have been a failure if he had pursued music and not cricket. If Nadal had become a businessman, the world would have lost an outstanding tennis player and he would, perhaps, not have been successful at business. If A.R. Rahman had joined an engineering college, he may have wallowed in mediocrity. He is world famous because he chose the area of his passion. Albert Einstein wrote, 'Everybody is a genius. But if you judge a fish by its ability to climb a tree, it will live its whole life believing that it is stupid.'

In the field of your svadharma, fix a higher goal. It is the thought of self that comes in the way of success. How not to think of yourself? Think of something beyond you. The law is, 'As you think so you become'. So far, you have thought only of yourself, your own body, mind and intellect and you have become a limited, restricted, small being. Fix a higher goal, a nobler cause. Espouse an ideal that is inclusive, not exclusive. One that is collective, not personal. Backed by an expanded vision, not a myopic view of things.

The human body is like the engine of a car. The more you act, the more energy you create. Work hard, work wholeheartedly for the goal. Love what you are doing. Be devoted to it with all your being.

The more inclusive the goal you surrender to, the greater is the energy you produce. Direct all your actions towards the objective you have set for yourself. Water flowing in one direction creates hydroelectric power. Wind moving in one direction produces energy. Similarly, thoughts directed to one goal create energy. The higher the goal, the greater the energy you generate.

Do not dissipate this energy by worrying over the past, feeling anxious about the future or getting into a frenzy in the present. Concentrate on the present action. Let the intellect direct the mind to the present action without meandering into the unproductive avenues of past worry or future anxiety. Then you will obtain success, the likes of which you scarce imagined! You will be happy. The law is that all selfish people are unhappy. Most importantly, your desires will reduce. You will grow to your potential.

The highest quality of action is selfless action, where you are driven neither by the desire to benefit yourself nor by the desire to work for others. You have only one goal – that of Enlightenment or self-realization. A lady makes prasad for a puja, and it turns out delicious. A few days later, her children ask her to make it again. The same lady makes the same dish with the same ingredients. This time it is not as tasty. On the day of the puja, she had made it for God. This crucial component was missing the second time around.

The movie *Chariots of Fire* is a historical film based on the true story of two athletes from Great Britain and Northern Ireland in the 1924 Olympics – Eric Liddell, a devout Scottish Christian, who runs for the glory of God, and Harold Abrahams, an English Jew who runs to overcome prejudice. In the 400m race, Liddell, known as the 'Flying Scotsman', said 'I ran the first 200m as quickly as I could and, with the help of God, I ran the next 200m even more strongly.' Liddell's time of 47.6 was an Olympic record, one that stood until Berlin 1936.

Anyone with the vision of the transcendental achieves miracles and obtains the goal of infinite happiness.

13

Path of Devotion

The second pathway to reduce desire is through the mind, by way of love. Today, your love is restricted to only yourself and perhaps the immediate family. Spread it to others. Include the extended family, society, fellow countrymen, the whole world in your circle of love. Feel for them. Be considerate towards them. Put yourself in their shoes. Empathize with them.

Have you wondered why you seem to have conflict with the people you love most? Why do the days of wine and roses soon become days of whine and neuroses? This is because of attachment. Attachment is love plus selfishness. Today, the love you feel is tainted with selfishness. It is conditional to a return. You have expectations from your loved ones. You make demands on them. When these expectations and demands are not met, you get angry and there is frustration, bitterness and discord in relationships.

The Bhagavad Gita extols the virtue of detachment. Detachment is not physical separation, but a state of mind. Detachment is unselfishness, which comes from self-sufficiency. If a person has had a fractured leg and is unable to stand on his legs, he needs a crutch. Another person may be able to stand on his own feet but has the luxury of leaning against a wall. Attachment is when you are like a creeper, with no strength to live by yourself. You need to lean on family and friends for support. When you gain inner strength and become independent, you no longer need to hang on to people for support. But you have the privilege of establishing wonderful relationships with a wide circle of people.

The entire world is strongly entrenched in feelings of separateness. It promotes competition, one-upmanship and discord. This leads to intolerance and inability to get along with people, because you take the stand, 'It's my way or the highway.' Ironically, it is these very people who are most dependent on others. Yet, they lack the ability to nurture lasting relationships and end up lonely and miserable.

The Bhagavad Gita speaks of oneness as the way to go. It helps cultivate cooperation, equality and accord. The adrenaline that comes with competition is replaced with the quiet strength of love. Where there is love, you see the best in others. You connect with them at their best. They, in turn, give their best. Everyone puts their best foot forward and you accomplish wondrous results.

In the poem titled 'The Nightingale and the Glow-worm' by William Cowper, a nightingale sings all day long, and as dusk approaches, he feels the pangs of hunger. He spots a glow-worm in the dark and is about to pounce on it and devour it, when the glow-worm realizes what is happening. He addresses the Nightingale:

'Did you admire my lamp,' quoth he,
'As much as I your minstrelsy,
You would abhor to do me wrong,
As much as I to spoil your song,

For 'twas the self-same power divine
Taught you to sing, and me to shine,
That you with music, I with light,
Might beautify and cheer the night.'

The Nightingale lets go of the worm!

When you feel one, you do not feel insecure or threatened. You do not imagine enemies outside and do not lash out at people in a vain attempt to protect yourself. While driving in India, if you get caught by a cop for a traffic violation you do not panic. You are not fearful. But if a cop in New York stops you for speeding, you are terrified because of the underlying feeling of otherness. You are on guard, get nervous and say the wrong things.

Love converts drudgery to revelry. When you have a difficult task on hand and you do it with a group of friends, the task gets done in an atmosphere of fun and cheer. The same job is painful if you have to do it by yourself.

In the 1950s and '60s, all food would be made at home, including difficult items such as papad and pickle. Papad-making was the highlight of summer vacations, when the ladies of the community would come together and papad would be made in a spirit of camaraderie, togetherness, joy, fun and laughter. Everyone was included – young and old – and each one was given a specific task to complete. When the feeling of oneness died out, papad-making stopped, and you now have to buy it from a store.

A wedding in the family was a fun event. The wedding planner, the performers at the *sangeet*, musical extravaganza, the preparation, organizing and implementation were all done in-house, among the members of the larger family. It was hard work but performed in a spirit of togetherness, which made for memorable occasions. When that spirit vanished everything turned commercial.

With oneness, you achieve success as you are able to build teams of people who go beyond the call of duty to achieve the shared goal. Your happiness multiplies. Today, you are jubilant only when good things happen to you. If your neighbour bags a huge contract or buys a luxury car, you are positively unhappy. Feel one with the neighbour. He has to work hard to achieve success and you celebrate as if the achievement was yours! Your desires reduce as you give priority to others' wishes over your own.

The highest state is when your love for human beings shifts to love for God. You pick a symbol of that Force and direct all your love towards that entity. You are aware of the bounty and abundance bestowed on you by the Divine Spirit. You are overcome with gratitude and surrender to that Being. This is devotion.

The Bhagavad Gita invites you to partake of the power of devotion. It draws you to experience a vitality that comes from identifying with the whole rather than just your little self. It takes you from a deeply entrenched position of antagonism to that of concern, understanding and respect. You move from feelings of isolation and loneliness to communication. And finally to communion with the Divine. You *become* God!

When you are body centric, you see maximum differences. You feel inimical towards people. Everyone is an opponent, including family members. As you identify with the mind, you begin to see unison within the family. It feels good to be home, where you do not need to be on guard.

Further, when any member of the family does well, you feel as if the achievement was yours.

Identify with the intellect, and your circle of oneness expands further still. If you are committed to the nation, all countrymen become yours. You revel in the variety of languages, customs, food and characteristics of different communities, be they Bengali, Punjabi, Gujarati, Tamil or Malayali. You celebrate the achievement of any Indian, anywhere in the world, as if it were yours. Thus, your happiness multiplies 1.3 billion times! At the international level, diversity has become a palpable goal to strive for and achieve. We savour the cuisine of various cultures, adopt their ways and enjoy the variety. Feel one with the whole world and your happiness multiplies by the trillions.

There was once a king who had a room full of mirrors. He would enter the mirror room before he went to his durbar just to ensure that he was presentable. Only the king had access to the mirror room. Once, the servant forgot to lock the room after the king left. The royal dog, the only dog in the palace, entered the mirror room. He was appalled to see so many dogs out there in the mirrors. He felt threatened and barked at the dogs. To his horror, they barked back at him. He snarled and growled. They responded in like manner. In the end, he attacked the other dogs and by the time the king returned from his court the dog was lying in a pool of blood, dead. The message to us is – live like a king, not a dog!

If you bark at people, they will only bark back at you. Attack them and they will attack you in return. Have the royal vision, which sees all beings as reflections of your own self and not as competitors. Admire yourself in them. Marvel at them. Include them in your circle of love.

The final step is the move to the Spirit. Then all differences and demarcations break down. You embrace the entire universe with love. The *Ishavasya Upanishad* says, 'One who sees the Self in all beings and all beings in the Self feels no hatred or revulsion.' Then where is the sorrow or delusion for the seer of oneness? You see Divinity everywhere and become one with It.

When a ray of white light is passed through a prism, it gets refracted into seven distinct and different colours. You enjoy the variety of colours, but you understand they sprang from the one ray of white light. Similarly, you are looking at the world through the prism of the body and its preferences, the mind and its loves and hates, and the intellect with its biases and prejudices. Reduce the sharp opposites and the prism will become a thin sheet. Then you will see unity in the diversity of beings everywhere. You will be free from hatred, sorrow and delusion. You will be in bliss all the time. You will merge with the Spirit.

14

Path of Knowledge

Knowledge is the only antidote to ignorance. All of humanity is steeped in ignorance. You have no idea where you have come from, or where you will go once your sojourn in this world is over. You do not know when you will depart from the world. You do not know what the purpose of your existence is. You have no clue how to live life such that you obtain what you want. You are seeking happiness. You do not know where it lies or how to gain it. Yet, you fancy yourself as intelligent!

If you have to find your watch in a beautifully decorated room that is dark, you will inadvertently knock your knee against a piece of furniture, trip over something or send something else flying. You will have a painful, unpleasant experience in the room, and might still not find what you are looking for. So, you rearrange the furniture, buy new items, remove some. Nothing helps as the room is still dark. All you need is light. Then you will be able to find your way around all the objects in the room and find your watch.

Similarly, you are trying to find happiness in the world in complete darkness, ignorance. All you get is stress and misery interspersed with a few moments of joy. So, you try and rearrange the world and improve it. Science and technology have enabled us to vastly improve the world. Yet, the problems persist. You need just a little knowledge. Knowledge of the nature of the world, your disposition and the technique of right contact with the world. You find happiness as you are, wherever you may be.

We are spending years of research and billions of dollars in making the world a better place. Yet, because this crucial piece of knowledge is missing, you find billionaires in depression, the most brilliant scientists and economists unhappy, and everyone chasing after a mirage.

Ancient masters in India understood this and had as the subject of their research the human mind. They laid down knowledge that will enable us to achieve success in the world, happiness within and growth to our potential.

Ignorance is the main problem. You want success. You do everything that results in failure. You seek wonderful relationships. You choose smooth talkers, who work against you. Even if you find the right person, you get attached and possessive and ruin the relationship. Thus, you end up in a hell of your own making.

The Bhagavad Gita gives you the knowledge of the world and how it functions. It places a mirror before you so you know yourself. And it teaches the technique of dealing with the world. Then, life becomes simple. You get what you want. Effortlessly, easily, with no stress. Most importantly, you gain happiness.

Knowledge does not mean mastery over the scriptures and their contents. It is, as Adi Shankaracharya puts it, *nitya anitya viveka vichara*

– reflection on the distinction between the permanent and the impermanent. It is the wisdom to understand that everything in the world passes and that it is unintelligent to depend on transient, trivial things of the world. Then, the search for the permanent begins.

Biochemistry tells us that the cells in our body have a limited life span, from days to weeks, or a few years. They are replaced regularly and we have a constantly changing body. However, our consciousness of who we are remains the same. Similarly, the mind changes. Emotions, likes and dislikes, loves and hates change as we go along. A person you loved some time back becomes your worst enemy and vice versa. The intellect and its concepts, ideas and ideologies also transform. A communist turns capitalist, your world view changes. The subtle intellect or conscience undergoes transformation. What you thought was right five years ago appears totally wrong. Meat eaters turn vegan when their conscience awakens to the cruelty meted out to animals. However, the 'I' factor remains constant and uniform through these variations.

Even though we change in our body, likes and dislikes and thinking over the years, there is an unchanging factor against which we recognize the changes happening within. That one unchanging 'I' cannot be equal to the many varying factors. Then what is this 'I'? Who are you?

In life, there is the case of mistaken identity. You wrongly believe yourself to be the body, mind and intellect. The 'I' is your real personality, unchanging and immortal. Adi Shankaracharya, in *Atmabodha*, says, '*Atma tu satatam praptah*' – Atman, your real Self, the 'I', is an ever-present reality. It never deserts you. It never abandons you. It is your real identity. The physical, emotional, intellectual identity you have assumed is a false imposition. Shed it. Shake it off. And you regain your true identity.

What is Atman? How do you connect with it? Pause, think, reflect. When was the last time you gazed at the sunrise or sunset and wondered who made the sun? Who or what placed the sun at the right distance from the earth to sustain life? Who makes the earth rotate around its axis and revolve around the sun meticulously? Who made the marvel of a heart that nurtures life? Who made the spleen, kidneys, liver, etc., that perform their roles perfectly without breakdowns or annual maintenance? You can go on and on.

You may not know the answers to these questions, but just the questions put you in a state of wonderment, amazement and admiration. That unknown power is God, Atman. The same power that enables you to see, hear, smell, taste and touch; the force that enlivens every emotion you entertain and every thought you think.

When people asked these questions, the answer they were given was that God makes all this happen. And most people went back satisfied. But that is like working on a mathematical problem with – let the answer be x. X is not the answer. It is only the first step to finding the solution. You have to work on it and derive the answer. Similarly, saying God created the world is like saying let the answer be x. You have to work dedicatedly to find the answer.

Thus, the search for the permanent begins. You are no longer satisfied with the trivial, insignificant things of the world. You begin to look within. The Bhagavad Gita gives you knowledge of yourself.

It introduces you to yourself – to your own inner components.

Knowledge lends clarity of thought, with which you become a sharp, creative thinker. This leads to success. You are happy as you are no longer resting on the impermanent aspects of life. You tap into deeper sources of happiness in you. And desires for the world get replaced by the one all-consuming desire for Truth.

All living beings are in the pursuit of happiness. Yet, nobody seems to have found it. The Bhagavad Gita gives the formula for happiness by which everyone can gain infinite Bliss. The formula is:

$$\text{HAPPINESS} = \frac{\text{DESIRES FULFILLED}}{\text{DESIRES HARBOURED}}$$

Using this formula, if you want to increase your happiness, you need to either increase the numerator or decrease the denominator. That is, either increase the desires you fulfil or reduce the desires you entertain. Most people focus on the numerator. We are all on a mission to fulfil more and more desires. The external system has done its bit to maximize this.

Before the age of credit cards and creative financial solutions, if you did not have money to buy that dream house or luxury car, you had no option but to drink a glass of cold water and go to sleep. Today, we are in the age of instant gratification. So you buy now, pay later. With this, the numerator goes up exponentially, but happiness remains the same or actually goes down. This is because as you fulfil desires, more are created. While the numerator goes up the denominator is also increasing, at a faster rate.

Even mathematically, the numerator is irrelevant. If you shift your focus to the denominator and reduce the desires you have, your happiness increases in leaps and bounds. And if you bring the denominator down to zero, you get infinite happiness. This is what all human beings are seeking. You will never achieve this as long as you are obsessed with the numerator.

Thus, if you are serious about gaining happiness, it calls for a significant shift away from chasing after desire to reducing the desire load you are carrying. How does one do that? You cannot give up desire. Nobody can give up desire. You can only take up a higher desire, one that is more fulfilling, captivating, gratifying.

Flashback to your childhood. As a child, you had millions of desires for toys and playthings. Do you still have the same desires? Did you at any stage make a decision to give up those desires? Then how did they go away? You merely grew to appreciate higher, more exciting things. When you were excited about riding a bicycle, toys vanished of their own accord. When you were introduced to the thrills of teenage life, all playthings disappeared. Thus, you moved to more enchanting things and as you grew, the lower enjoyments were found wanting.

As adults, we are all spiritual kids! We are stuck with material and physical attractions. Move to emotional fascinations, and physical desires will drop. A mother who is offered her favourite chocolate prefers to give it to her child instead. The emotional joy of seeing the child enjoy the chocolate is so great that the physical desire of wanting the chocolate vanishes.

Go up one more stage to the intellectual level and even emotional joys fade into insignificance. A scientist on the verge of discovering a vaccine for the novel coronavirus is indifferent to physical comforts and rises above emotional attachments too.

Take that giant leap into the realm of the Spirit and all worldly desires drop. You gain access to the realm of the infinite. Once you gain infinite happiness, nothing can be taken away from you or be added to you. Infinite plus a million is still infinite. Infinite plus infinite is also infinite. Infinite minus a billion is infinite and infinite minus infinite is not zero, but still infinite! You have accomplished your life's mission. Thereafter, there is nothing you need. You are no longer dependent on the vagaries of the world. You are all-blissful, all-powerful, all-loving!

15

Meditation and Enlightenment

The three pathways should be practised as per your constitution. If you tend to be more active, you will naturally gravitate towards Karma Yoga, the path of action. A person who is emotional will instinctively move to Bhakti Yoga, the path of devotion, and an intellectual will go for Jnana Yoga, the path of knowledge. However, if you want to make quick progress, all three must be practised in line with your nature. Then, there will be a meteoric rise in your personality. You will be more cheerful, less affected by the changes in the world and free from sorrow. You will then be left with only a few desires – to get to freedom, to give back to the guru who taught you this invaluable knowledge and to serve the world. You become meditative. Your thoughts are anchored in Atman, even while you are engaged with the world. You then practise meditation.

Meditation is the technique of focusing on one thought without allowing the mind to meander to any other thought, under the supervision of the intellect. Theoretically, that one thought could be anything, but in practice, it helps if you choose a mantra of your liking. 'Om' is the most powerful symbol of Atman. It is a popular mantra, which has no association with anything in the world.

It is a universal mantra, not restricted to any particular faith. It is not even a Sanskrit word as it is not subject to its declensions or grammatical rules. The very sound of Om is soothing. And it has a deep significance. The word 'Om' comes from three letters of the alphabet – A, U and M. They cover all sound as there is no sound before A, which is guttural, and no sound after M which is labial. These three represent the waking, dream and deep-sleep states we all go through. The silence that supports all sound represents Atman.

As you go into deep meditation, you stop the chant. When the last thought goes, the mind becomes extinct as the mind is only a flow of thoughts. The intellect, which distinguishes between the sound and silence, now has no job. It gets stuck in the silence and goes away. When the mind and intellect go, only Atman remains. Your individuality has gone, but you have merged with the totality. The artificial distinctions of name and form have gone.

Once you reach the state of Enlightenment, you are above the Law of Karma. Nothing you do leaves a footprint as you are free from desire. You continue to live because of the momentum of past desires. Just as a car moving at 100 miles per hour does not stop abruptly when the ignition is switched off, rolling for a while before it comes to a halt. In the interim, there is no acceleration. The movement comes from the velocity of the past. Similarly, all enlightened souls live for a while, driven by the momentum of their past desires.

It is this period that is most valuable for those of us who want to get to that state. We draw inspiration from their mere presence and their teachings help us remove the veil of delusion and cloud of desire and ego. We find ourselves and, in turn, guide the next generation. This is the unbroken *guru-shishya parampara*, the mentor-protégé lineage, which has been in India since time immemorial.

ABOUT THE AUTHOR

Jaya Row is one of the most powerful speakers on Vedanta. Well-loved and popular as an inspiring spiritual leader, her expositions on Vedanta touch the mind and uplift the intellect. Backed by her experience in the corporate world and forty years of research on Vedanta, she motivates her audiences to live successful and happy lives. Clarity, wit and zeal are the hallmarks of her presentations.

She has gained international recognition, having spoken at prestigious forums such as the World Economic Forum, Davos, World Bank, Young

Presidents' Organization, Princeton University, Purdue University, Washington University as well as the leading corporate organisations of the world.